WHO'S WHO OF PRO SPORTS

WHO'S WHO OF
PRO
BASKETBALL

A GUIDE TO THE GAME'S GREATEST PLAYERS

by Tyler Omoth

CAPSTONE PRESS
a capstone imprint

Sports Illustrated Kids Who's Who of Pro Sports are published by Capstone Press,
1710 Roe Crest Drive, North Mankato, Minnesota 56003
www.capstonepub.com

Library of Congress Cataloging-in-Publication Data
Omoth, Tyler.
  Who's who of pro basketball : a guide to the game's greatest players / by Tyler Omoth.
      pages cm.—(Sports Illustrated Kids. Who's Who of Pro Sports.)
  Includes bibliographical references and index.
  Summary: "Introduces readers to the most dynamic pro basketball stars of today and yesterday, including
notable statistics and records"—Provided by publisher.
  Audience: Age: 9-10.
  Audience: Grade: 4 to 6.
  ISBN 978-1-62065-926-7 (library binding)
  ISBN 978-1-4914-7607-9 (eBook PDF)
  1. Basketball players—Biography—Juvenile literature. 2. Basketball players—Rating of—Juvenile
literature. I. Title.
  GV884.A1O66 2016
  796.323092′2—dc23
  [B]
                          2015002809

Editorial Credits
Nate LeBoutillier, editor; Kyle Grenz, designer; Eric Gohl, media researcher

Photo Credits
Corbis: Bettmann, 22; Getty Images/NBAE: David Sherman, 15, Dick Raphael, 27; Newscom: Cal Sport
Media/Chris Szagola, 20, EFE/Craig Lassig, 13, EPA/Jason Szenes, 9 (bottom), Icon SMI/Jeff Lewis, 14;
Shutterstock: B Calkins, 6; Sports Illustrated: Al Tielemans, 5, 8, Andy Hayt, 21, 26, Bob Rosato, 10 (bottom),
David E. Klutho, 11, 17 (top), Hy Peskin, 24, John Biever, 9 (top), 16, John G. Zimmerman, cover (left), 19
(top), John W. McDonough, cover (middle), 4, 7, 10 (top), 12 (all), 17 (bottom), 23 (right), 25, Manny Millan,
cover (right), 19 (bottom), 23 (left), 28, Walter Iooss Jr., 18

Design Elements: Shutterstock

Printed in the United States of America in North Mankato, Minnesota.
042015   008823CGF15

TABLE OF CONTENTS

BEST
OF THE BEST

Fans love the National Basketball Association (NBA) for its high-flying dunks, buzzer-beating shots, and spectacular passes. All NBA players are great athletes. They're the best in the world at what they do. Some players soar for rim-rocking slams while others flip unbelievable no-look passes. Some players defend the basket with majestic shot blocks while others excel at tossing rainbow jump shots into the hoop. However, even among these dynamite athletes, some stand out above the rest. The pages to come will showcase spectacular players you don't want to miss and won't soon forget.

STEPHEN **CURRY**

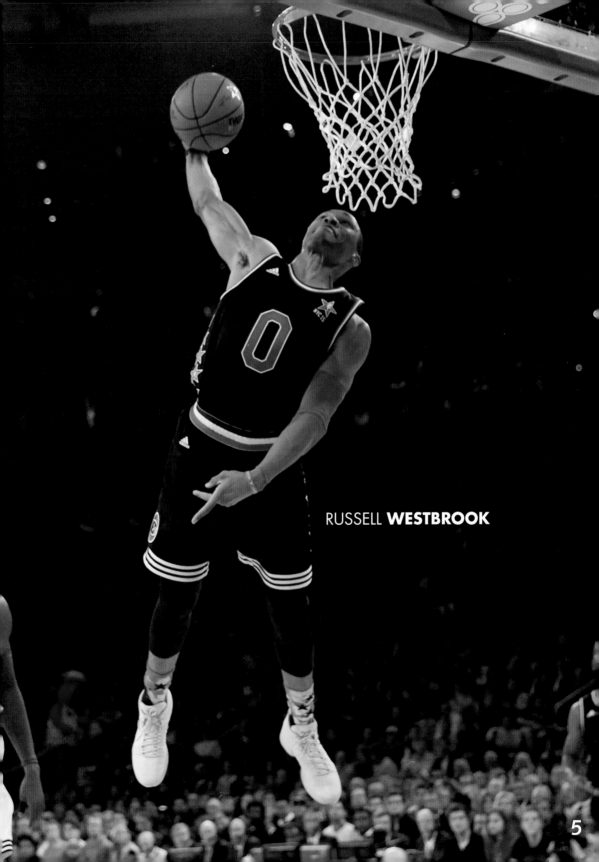

RUSSELL **WESTBROOK**

GREATS

Modern-Day MVPs

Check out this list of the most valuable players (MVPs) from the past 15 NBA seasons.

Year:	Most Valuable Player:
2000–01	Allen **Iverson**, guard, Philadelphia 76ers
2001–02	Tim **Duncan**, forward, San Antonio Spurs
2002–03	Tim **Duncan**, forward, San Antonio Spurs
2003–04	Kevin **Garnett**, forward, Minnesota Timberwolves
2004–05	Steve **Nash**, guard, Phoenix Suns
2005–06	Steve **Nash**, guard, Phoenix Suns
2006–07	Dirk **Nowitzki**, forward, Dallas Mavericks
2007–08	Kobe **Bryant**, guard, Los Angeles Lakers
2008–09	LeBron **James**, forward, Cleveland Cavaliers
2009–10	LeBron **James**, forward, Cleveland Cavaliers
2010–11	Derrick **Rose**, guard, Chicago Bulls
2011–12	LeBron **James**, forward, Miami Heat
2012–13	LeBron **James**, forward, Miami Heat
2013–14	Kevin **Durant**, forward, Oklahoma City Thunder
2014–15	Stephen **Curry**, guard Golden State Warriors

REMARKABLE RECORDS

Kareem Abdul-Jabbar holds the record for most MVP awards with six.

Big Name, Big Game

KEVIN **DURANT**

Tall and spindly, Kevin Durant hardly looks tough enough to be a pro athlete. But in 2009–2010, he won his first league scoring title at just 21 years old, making him the youngest to ever pull off the feat. By the age of 24, he'd already been an NBA All-Star six times, the league scoring champion four times, the All-Star Game MVP, and the NBA's MVP. With deceptive quickness and a graceful shooting stroke, Durant may be a big name with big game in the NBA for a long time to come.

STAT-TASTIC

In 2013–14 Kevin Durant scored 40 or more points 13 times. His best effort was a 62-point game against the Atlanta Hawks.

High Shine

The NBA holds its All-Star game each year at mid-season. The players selected make up an annual "Who's Who" of basketball each year. The rosters at the 2015 NBA All-Star Game featured shining stars from top to bottom. Did your favorite player make the list?

2015 Western Conference All-Stars

No.	Name	Team	Pos.	Ht.	Wt.
30	*Stephen **Curry**	Golden State Warriors	G	6-3	190
13	*James **Harden**	Houston Rockets	G	6-5	225
11	*Klay **Thompson**	Golden State Warriors	G	6-7	215
12	*LaMarcus **Aldridge**	Portland Trail Blazers	F	6-11	240
33	*Marc **Gasol**	Memphis Grizzlies	C	7-1	265
15	DeMarcus **Cousins**	Sacramento Kings	C	6-11	270
0	Russell **Westbrook**	Oklahoma City Thunder	G	6-3	200
21	Tim **Duncan**	San Antonio Spurs	F	6-11	250
35	Kevin **Durant**	Oklahoma City Thunder	G	6-9	240
0	Damian **Lillard**	Portland Trail Blazers	G	6-3	195
41	Dirk **Nowitzki**	Dallas Mavericks	F	7-0	245
3	Chris **Paul**	Los Angeles Clippers	G	6-0	175
32	Blake **Griffin**	Los Angeles Clippers	F	6-10	251
24	Kobe **Bryant**	Los Angeles Lakers	G	6-6	212
23	Anthony **Davis**	New Orleans Pelicans	C	6-10	220
	Steve **Kerr**	Golden State Warriors		Coach	

*denotes starter

2015 Eastern Conference All-Stars

No.	Name	Team	Pos.	Ht.	Wt.
2	*John **Wall**	Washington Wizards	G	6-4	195
7	*Kyle **Lowry**	Toronto Raptors	G	6-0	205
23	*LeBron **James**	Cleveland Cavaliers	F	6-8	250
7	*Carmelo **Anthony**	New York Knicks	F	6-8	240
16	*Pau **Gasol**	Chicago Bulls	C	7-0	250
1	Chris **Bosh**	Miami Heat	C	6-11	235
21	Jimmy **Butler**	Chicago Bulls	G	6-7	220
15	Al **Horford**	Atlanta Hawks	F	6-10	250
2	Kyrie **Irving**	Cleveland Cavaliers	G	6-3	193
26	Kyle **Korver**	Atlanta Hawks	G	6-7	212
4	Paul **Millsap**	Atlanta Hawks	F	6-8	253
0	Jeff **Teague**	Atlanta Hawks	G	6-2	181
3	Dwyane **Wade**	Miami Heat	G	6-4	220
	Mike **Budenholzer**	Atlanta Hawks		Coach	

LEBRON **JAMES**

STAT-TASTIC

In 2015 Kobe Bryant was selected to his 17th All-Star game, and Tim Duncan was selected to his 15th game. Kareem Abdul-Jabbar was selected to 19 All-Star games, the most ever.

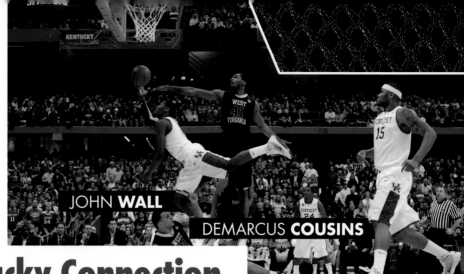

JOHN **WALL**

DEMARCUS **COUSINS**

Kentucky Connection

John Wall and DeMarcus Cousins were opponents in the 2015 NBA All-Star Game. But the pair were Kentucky Wildcats teammates in college for the 2009–2010 basketball season. This "Kentucky Connection" is nothing new in the NBA. From 1947 to 2015, 85 Kentucky University student-athletes have played in the NBA or ABA (American Basketball Association). In 2014 alone, no less than 24 Kentucky alumni were active players in the NBA. Unsurprisingly, talent like that has helped the Wildcats to more wins than any other college program.

REMARKABLE RECORDS

PAU (16) AND
MARC (33) **GASOL**

The opening tip of the 2015 NBA All-Star game was contested by brothers for the first time ever. Older brother Pau Gasol of the Eastern Conference won the jump ball over Marc Gasol of the Western Conference.

Grizzly Grinder

It's the fourth quarter of a close game. The point guard dribbles around a screen, hoping for an open shot. Memphis Grizzlies big man Marc Gasol, however, is there to stop him. Gasol blocks the shot, grabs the ball, and tosses the outlet pass for the fast break. That's the kind of focus and intensity Gasol brings to the table. The Grizzlies' Man in the Middle was NBA Defensive Player of the Year in 2012–13 and makes his team one of the toughest in the league on D.

MARC **GASOL**

JOHN **STOCKTON**

REMARKABLE RECORDS

John Stockton tallied 3,265 steals in a 19-year NBA career. Next best on the list is Jason Kidd, who also played 19 NBA seasons but made 581 fewer steals.

Mr. Relentless

A blur of wild hair and intensity, Joakim Noah is relentless on defense. He stays between his man and the hoop at all times and will sacrifice his body to take a charge. If a ball gets loose, Noah scrambles to scoop it up. The 2013–14 NBA Defensive Player of the Year never relaxes on the court.

JOAKIM **NOAH**

STAT-TASTIC

Joakim Noah played college basketball at the University of Florida. In his three seasons as a Gator, he averaged 10.5 points and 6.4 rebounds per game. He helped his teams to two national titles.

11

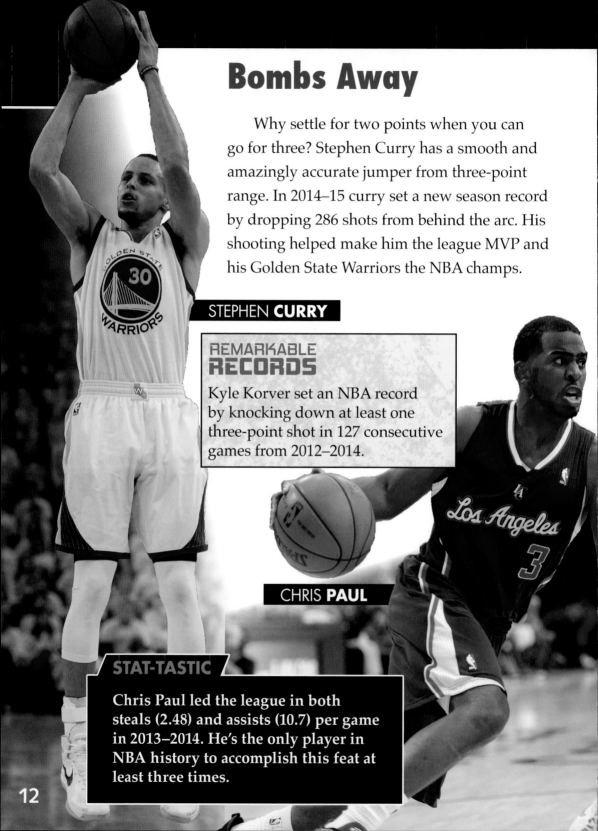

Bombs Away

Why settle for two points when you can go for three? Stephen Curry has a smooth and amazingly accurate jumper from three-point range. In 2014–15 curry set a new season record by dropping 286 shots from behind the arc. His shooting helped make him the league MVP and his Golden State Warriors the NBA champs.

STEPHEN **CURRY**

REMARKABLE RECORDS

Kyle Korver set an NBA record by knocking down at least one three-point shot in 127 consecutive games from 2012–2014.

CHRIS **PAUL**

STAT-TASTIC

Chris Paul led the league in both steals (2.48) and assists (10.7) per game in 2013–2014. He's the only player in NBA history to accomplish this feat at least three times.

Pass Master

Blink and you'll miss it. Like a magician performing a slight-of-hand trick, the best NBA players get the ball to teammates in amazing ways. Guards like Minnesota Timberwolf Ricky Rubio bounce passes between defenders' legs, dish tasty no-looks, fling end-to-end bombs, and lob highlight-friendly alley-oops.

Chairmen of the Boards

A good rebounder's instincts and determination make him a monster on the boards. Footwork, positioning, technique, and leaping ability also help. Los Angeles Clippers big man DeAndre Jordan snagged an NBA-best 15 rebounds per game in 2014–15. Other active seasonal league-leaders include Kevin Love, Dwight Howard, and Kevin Garnett.

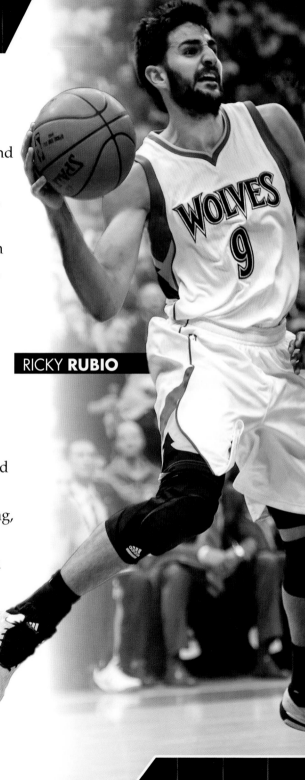

RICKY **RUBIO**

Bryant's Burst

On January 22, 2006, the Toronto
Raptors led the Los Angeles Lakers by
18 points in the third quarter. Then Laker
shooting guard Kobe Bryant dialed up
his game. He led his team to a comeback
victory by scoring 57 of his astounding
81 total points in the second half. An
amazing scorer, Bryant has scored more
than 60 points five times in his career.
On December 14, 2014, Bryant passed
Michael Jordan for third place on the
all-time scoring list.

STAT-TASTIC

Bill Russell scored 30 points and
grabbed 40 rebounds in Game 7 of
the 1962 Finals against the Lakers.
No one else has had a 40-rebound
game in Finals history.

Double the Love

KEVIN **LOVE**

On November 12, 2010, Kevin Love helped the Minnesota Timberwolves turn what looked like it would be a loss into a win. Love ripped down 31 rebounds and scored 31 points to secure the NBA's first 30-30 game since 1982 when Moses Malone did it. Love did most of his damage in the third quarter, with Minnesota down 21 points. Love continued to dominate in the fourth quarter, leading the Timberwolves to a 112–103 comeback victory.

REMARKABLE RECORDS

On May 17, 2011, Dallas Maverick's star Dirk Nowitzki set the mark for most free throws without a miss in a playoff game. He went 24 for 24 from the free throw line.

Big Ticket

In 1995 Kevin Garnett came into the NBA as a gangly 19-year-old. He fully grew into the role of amazing NBA player by capturing the NBA's MVP honors in 2004. Off the court Garnett is known as a great teammate. On the court, he's intense, animated, trash-talking, and sometimes just plain silly. Sometimes, on defense, he's even gotten down on all fours and howled like a wolf.

KEVIN **GARNETT**

Birdman

With a mohawk haircut, a scraggly beard, and lots of tattoos, Chris Andersen looks as colorful as his personality. He uses those long arms to block a lot of shots—occasionally even flapping his arms after a big play like a bird! The Miami Heat certainly liked Birdman's style during the 2012–13 season. A big part of Miami's title run was Anderson's steady role as back-up center ... and human energy boost!

CHRIS **ANDERSEN**

REMARKABLE RECORDS

On January 16th, 2015, LeBron James reached 24,000 points for his career. At just 30 years and 17 days old, he became the youngest player in NBA history to reach this milestone.

JAVALE **MCGEE**

Pierre McDunk

When seven-foot (2.13-meter) center JaVale McGee holds his finger mustache up to his face, he goes by the alter ego of Pierre McDunk. On the court, his boisterous personality shows through with sweeping dunks, emphatic blocks and laughable bloopers. Off the court, his social media accounts are among the funniest in all of sports. McGee's mother Pamela played two seasons in the Women's National Basketball Association (WNBA).

All-Time Team

To make it to the NBA at all, you must be great. The following list of players and coaches, then, would make a greatest of the great list.

Shooting Guard	Michael **Jordan**—"Air" Jordan dominated the league as an elite scorer, high-flying marvel, and competitive force. Jerry **West**—"The Logo" could can jumpers from anywhere, score in the clutch, and play lock-down defense. George **Gervin**—"The Iceman" defined the word "smooth" and made scoring look easy with silky jumpers and finger rolls.
Point Guard	Earvin "Magic" **Johnson**—This legend ran the floor like a deer, drove the lane like a truck,.and threw passes like a warlock. Oscar **Robertson**—The "Big-O" was the original "all-around" player, gathering triple-doubles like a champ. John **Stockton**—Mr. Give and Take holds NBA career records for both assists and steals.
Small Forward	Larry **Bird**—"Larry Legend" could conjure a bucket out of thin air with his never-before-seen shotmaking and clutch playmaking. Elgin **Baylor**—Small for the position, his running bank shot was nonetheless unstoppable. John **Havlicek**—This gritty player's constant motor made him a force on defense and a teammate unparalleled.

JOHN **HAVLICEK**

STAT-TASTIC

Magic Johnson had 30 triple doubles in the playoffs alone. LeBron James is the only active player to have more than 30 triple doubles in his entire career.

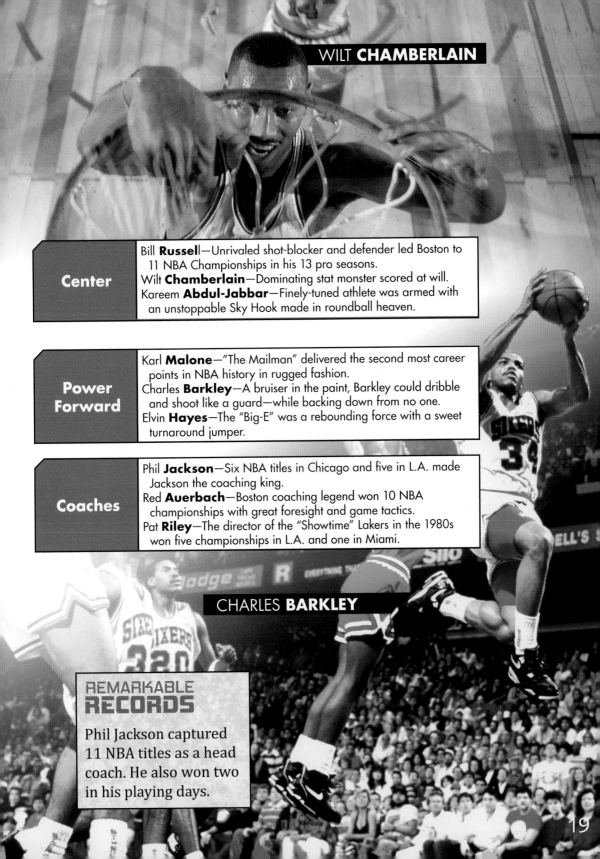

WILT CHAMBERLAIN

Center	Bill **Russell**—Unrivaled shot-blocker and defender led Boston to 11 NBA Championships in his 13 pro seasons. Wilt **Chamberlain**—Dominating stat monster scored at will. Kareem **Abdul-Jabbar**—Finely-tuned athlete was armed with an unstoppable Sky Hook made in roundball heaven.
Power Forward	Karl **Malone**—"The Mailman" delivered the second most career points in NBA history in rugged fashion. Charles **Barkley**—A bruiser in the paint, Barkley could dribble and shoot like a guard—while backing down from no one. Elvin **Hayes**—The "Big-E" was a rebounding force with a sweet turnaround jumper.
Coaches	Phil **Jackson**—Six NBA titles in Chicago and five in L.A. made Jackson the coaching king. Red **Auerbach**—Boston coaching legend won 10 NBA championships with great foresight and game tactics. Pat **Riley**—The director of the "Showtime" Lakers in the 1980s won five championships in L.A. and one in Miami.

CHARLES BARKLEY

REMARKABLE RECORDS

Phil Jackson captured 11 NBA titles as a head coach. He also won two in his playing days.

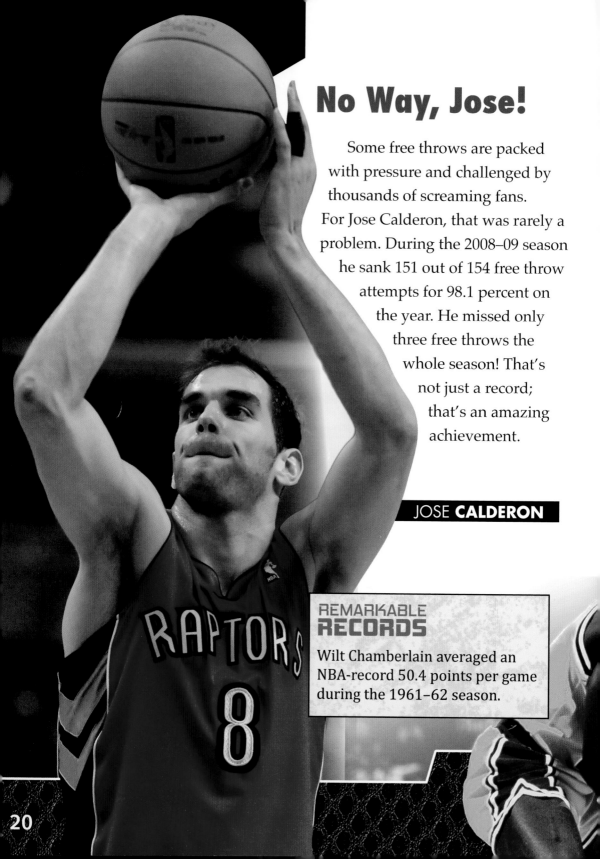

No Way, Jose!

Some free throws are packed with pressure and challenged by thousands of screaming fans. For Jose Calderon, that was rarely a problem. During the 2008–09 season he sank 151 out of 154 free throw attempts for 98.1 percent on the year. He missed only three free throws the whole season! That's not just a record; that's an amazing achievement.

JOSE **CALDERON**

REMARKABLE RECORDS

Wilt Chamberlain averaged an NBA-record 50.4 points per game during the 1961–62 season.

Other Amazing Achievements

• Scott **Skiles** dished out a generous total of 30 assists in a single game for the Orlando Magic on December 30, 1990.

• Oscar **Robertson** didn't just get a lucky few triple-doubles, he averaged double digits in scoring, assists, and rebounds for the entire 1961–62 season.

• Wilt **Chamberlain** racked up an astounding 100 points in a single game for the Philadelphia Warriors on March 2, 1962.

• Basketball's Iron Man, A.C. **Green** played in 1,192 consecutive games from November 19, 1986 to April 18, 2001.

• Kareem **Abdul-Jabbar** had a very long and productive career. He finished as the all-time leader in points scored with 38,387.

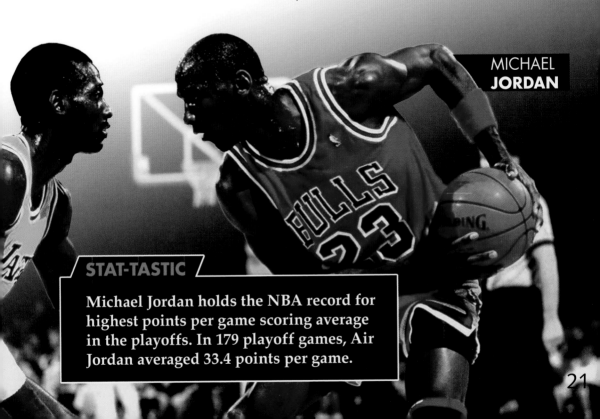

MICHAEL
JORDAN

STAT-TASTIC

Michael Jordan holds the NBA record for highest points per game scoring average in the playoffs. In 179 playoff games, Air Jordan averaged 33.4 points per game.

Greats by Era

Since basketball was invented in 1891, there have been many changes in the game. Here's a list of men who took the game to its highest levels through the ages.

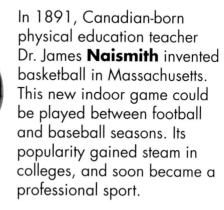

In 1891, Canadian-born physical education teacher Dr. James **Naismith** invented basketball in Massachusetts. This new indoor game could be played between football and baseball seasons. Its popularity gained steam in colleges, and soon became a professional sport.

1930s—Glenn **Roberts** changed the game forever by inventing the jump shot. Other early jump-shooters were Whitey **Skoog** and Kenny **Sailors**. Basketball first appeared as an Olympic sport at the 1936 Games in Berlin, Germany.

1940s—"Jumpin' Joe" **Fulks** and hip-shooting Fred **Scolari** dominated hoops in the 1940s.

1950s—Giant center George **Mikan**, guard Bob **Pettit**, and throwback forward Dolph **Schayes** ushered in the era of the NBA.

JAMES **NAISMITH**

STAT-TASTIC

The first NBA 3-point shot made was by Chris Ford of the Boston Celtics on October 12, 1979.

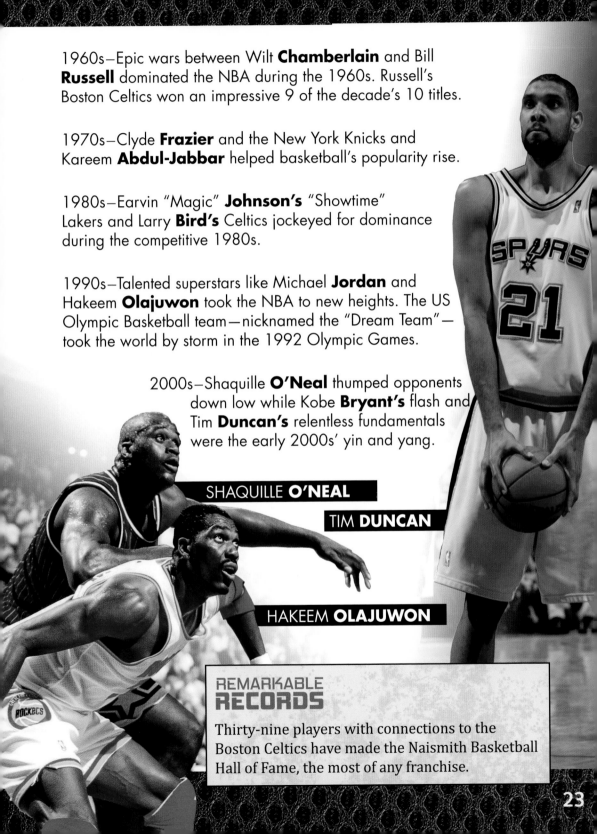

1960s—Epic wars between Wilt **Chamberlain** and Bill **Russell** dominated the NBA during the 1960s. Russell's Boston Celtics won an impressive 9 of the decade's 10 titles.

1970s—Clyde **Frazier** and the New York Knicks and Kareem **Abdul-Jabbar** helped basketball's popularity rise.

1980s—Earvin "Magic" **Johnson's** "Showtime" Lakers and Larry **Bird's** Celtics jockeyed for dominance during the competitive 1980s.

1990s—Talented superstars like Michael **Jordan** and Hakeem **Olajuwon** took the NBA to new heights. The US Olympic Basketball team—nicknamed the "Dream Team"—took the world by storm in the 1992 Olympic Games.

2000s—Shaquille **O'Neal** thumped opponents down low while Kobe **Bryant's** flash and Tim **Duncan's** relentless fundamentals were the early 2000s' yin and yang.

SHAQUILLE **O'NEAL**

TIM **DUNCAN**

HAKEEM **OLAJUWON**

REMARKABLE RECORDS

Thirty-nine players with connections to the Boston Celtics have made the Naismith Basketball Hall of Fame, the most of any franchise.

Chapter 3

TERRIFIC TEAMS

Hoops Dynasties

To build a sports dynasty takes great planning, hard work, and fantastic players. Here's a list of the most successful teams by era in the history of the NBA.

1950s Minneapolis Lakers

In the early days of the NBA, the Minneapolis Lakers were the dominant force. Led by big man George Mikan, the Lakers won five championships during the 1950s.

1960s Boston Celtics

Bill Russell and the Celtics won nine NBA titles during the 1960s. In all, the team won 11 titles in 13 years, making them one of the most dominant teams in sports history.

1980s Los Angeles Lakers

The "Showtime" Lakers of the 1980s were a fast-break team that made scoring look easy. Quarterbacked by legendary point guard Magic Johnson and anchored by Kareem Abdul-Jabbar, the Lakers were a force. Often more entertaining than Hollywood, the Lakers were a must-see team, garnering five NBA titles in the '80s.

1954 MINNEAPOLIS **LAKERS** VS. NEW YORK **KNICKS**

1990s Chicago Bulls

With Michael Jordan and Scottie Pippen leading the way, the 1995–96 Bulls set the mark for best-ever regular season record (72–10) on the way to their fourth of six championships in the '90s.

2000s San Antonio Spurs

The Tim Duncan era in San Antonio is a modern dynasty. Duncan's longtime running mates include point guard Tony Parker and forward Manu Ginobili, and an outstanding coach by the name of Gregg Popovich. The Spurs made the playoffs every year of the decade and won three NBA championships. They also won titles in 1999 and 2014 to bookend their greatness.

REMARKABLE RECORDS

The 1995–96 Chicago Bulls won 33 games on the road. That same season, eight other NBA teams failed to win 33 games *total*.

STAT-TASTIC

From 1959 to 1966 the Boston Celtics won a record eight consecutive NBA championships.

L.A. Glitz vs. Blue-Collar Boston

Magic Johnson and the L.A. Lakers were flashy and fast. Larry Bird's Boston Celtics were the blue-collar team that just kept winning. When the Lakers and the Celtics matched up, all eyes were on Magic and Bird, two all-time greats with completely different styles. Sometimes it's the personal rivalries that make team rivalries legendary. The two teams combined to win eight championships during the 1980s, matching up against each other in the Finals three times.

REMARKABLE RECORDS

The 1979 NCAA championship game was between Magic Johnson's Michigan State Spartans and Larry Bird's Indiana State Sycamores. It is still the highest-rated basketball broadcast in television history.

MAGIC **JOHNSON**

Battle of the Bigs

From 1959 to 1968 Wilt Chamberlain and Bill Russell each won the NBA MVP award four times. Two of the NBA's greatest players created one of the most intense personal rivalries in sports history. Like two heavyweight boxers, Russell and "The Big Dipper" banged and danced whenever their teams met. Wilt usually won the one-on-one battles, statistically.

But basketball is a team sport. And no center in the game's history was a better teammate than Russell, who balanced his all-around ability with firm leadership and a winning attitude. When all was said and done, Russell had more championship rings (11) than fingers.

STAT-TASTIC

Wilt Chamberlain averaged 30.1 points per game over his career, but only 23.2 points per game in his 51 tilts versus Russell.

BILL **RUSSELL** (6) AND WILT **CHAMBERLAIN** (13)

Best Ever?

Were the 1995–96 Bulls the best team in NBA history? The starting line-up featured NBA Hall of Famers Michael Jordan and Scottie Pippen as well as colorful rebounding fool Dennis Rodman, crafty point guard Ron Harper, and serviceable center Luc Longley. Off the bench came handy forward Toni Kukoc, sweet-shooting guard Steve Kerr, and a host of other solid vets. The Bulls went 72–10 in the regular season, including an impressive 39–2 home record. They swept the Eastern Conference Finals and beat the Seattle Supersonics four games to two in the Finals to cap their legendary season.

Celtic Mystique

The Boston Celtics have won more NBA championships (17) than any other franchise. Legendary dynasties like Bill Russell's teams in the 1960s and the Larry Bird's squad of the 1980s made Boston regular Finals champs. Paul Pierce, Ray Allen, and Kevin Garnett brought home their most recent trophy in 2008. Not surprisingly, the Celtics also have the most players in the Hall of Fame (39) and the most NBA MVP award winners (10).

STAT-TASTIC

The 1995–96 Bulls led the league with 105.2 points per game and gave up the the third fewest at 92.9 points per game. That's an average win by more than 12 points.

28

WONDERMENTS

Greatest Nicknames

Kevin Durant stalks the basketball court with long limbs and spider-like moves. This led some to nickname him "Durantula." Chris Bosh with his funny expression and thin shoulders and neck goes by "The Boshtrich." When you become a great in the NBA, you need a great nickname to go with it. Here are some of the best of the best, past and present.

Best Nicknames of Today	
Name	Nickname
Tim **Duncan**	"The Big Fundamental"
Nick **Young**	"Swaggy P"
Rafer **Alston**	"Skip 2 My Lou"
Derrick **Rose**	"Poohdini"
Dirk **Nowitzki**	"Dirkules"
Rudy **Gobert**	"The Stifle Tower"

Best Nicknames of Yesteryear	
Name	Nickname
Charles **Barkley**	"The Round Mound of Rebound"
Dominique **Wilkins**	"The Human Highlight Reel"
Bryant **Reeves**	"Big Country"
Sarunas **Jasikevicius**	"Jazzy Cabbages"

Greatest Records

Most wins in a season (72): Chicago **Bulls** 1995–96

Longest winning streak (33 games): Los Angeles **Lakers**, 1971–72

Only player to score 100 points in a game: Wilt **Chamberlain**

Highest points-per-game average, single season (50.4 ppg): Wilt **Chamberlain**,1961-62

Most NBA Finals MVP Awards (6): Michael **Jordan**,1961-62

Most career points (38,387): Kareem **Abdul-Jabbar**

Most career rebounds (23,924): Wilt **Chamberlain**

Most career assists (15,806): John **Stockton**

Consecutive games played (1,192): A.C. **Green**

Highest Field Goal Percentage, Career (.582): Shaquille **O'Neal**

Glossary

alley-oop (AHL-ee OOP)—pass thrown to a player who is running toward the basket and leaps to catch the pass in midair to dunk or lay the ball into the hoop

center (SEN-tuhr)—a basketball position; centers are usually the tallest players on the court and play closest to the basket

consecutive (kuhn-SEK-yuh-tiv)—when something happens several times in a row without a break

dominate (DAH-muh-nayt)—to rule; in sports, a team or person dominates if they win much more than anyone else

double-double—When a player has double figures (10 or more) in two statistical categories (i.e. 10 points and 10 rebounds)

dynasty (DYE-nuh-stee)—a team that wins multiple championships over a period of several years

forward (FORE-werd)—a basketball position; forwards are usually responsible for playing both close to or further from the basket

fundamental (fun-da-MEN-tuhl)—a basic part

guard (GARD)—a basketball position; guards are usually responsible for handling the ball, passing, and shooting from outside

outlet pass (OWT-let PASS)—a pass after a rebound or steal to a teammate to start a fast break

rivalry (RYE-val-ree)—a fierce feeling of competition between two teams

trash-talking (TRASH TAHLK)—insulting or boastful speech intended to demoralize an opponent or gain some sort of advantage

triple double—When a player has double figures (10 or more) in three statistical categories (i.e. 10 points, 10 rebounds and 10 assists)

Read More

Gitlin, Marty. *Playing Pro Basketball.* Playing Pro Sports. Minneapolis: Lerner Publications Co., 2015.

Kelley, K.C. *2014 Basketball Superstars.* NBA Readers. New York: Scholastic, 2014.

Lohre, Mike. *Six Degrees of LeBron James.* Six Degrees of Sports. North Mankato, Minn.: Capstone Press, 2015.

Internet Sites

FactHound offers a safe, fun way to find Internet sites related to this book. All of the sites on FactHound have been researched by our staff.

Here's all you do:

Visit *www.facthound.com*

Type in this code: 9781620659267

Check out projects, games and lots more at
www.capstonekids.com

Index